The Most
Extraordinary
Ordinary Day

Written by Jeanette Bonfiglio

Art by Shiela Alejandro

Illustrations by Sheila Alejandro
Cover & Layout by Praise Saflor

Publisher's Cataloging-in-Publication data

Names: Bonfiglio, Jeanette, author. | Alejandro, Shiela, illustrator.
Title: The Most Extraordinary Ordinary Day / Jeanette Bonfiglio ;
illustrated by Shiela Alejandro.
Description: Boca Raton, FL: Jeanette Bonfiglio, 2021. |
Summary: Amanda's day begins like any other... but in Amanda's imagination,
it quickly turns into an astonishing, spectacular, extraordinary day!
Identifiers: ISBN: 978-1-7333342-1-1 (hardcover) | 978-1-7333342-4-2 (paperback) |
978-1-7333342-5-9 (ebook)
Subjects: LCSH Imagination--Juvenile fiction. | Family--Juvenile fiction. |
CYAC Imagination--Fiction. | Family--Fiction. | BISAC JUVENILE FICTION / Imagination &
Play | JUVENILE FICTION / Family / Parents | JUVENILE FICTION / Fantasy & Magic
Classification: LCC PZ7.1.B66532 Mo 2021 | DDC [E]--dc23

For my daughter Amanda,
the inspiration for this story was born from your
vivid imagination that transformed my very
ordinary life into something *extraordinary*! – JB

"Hurry, Amanda," called Mommy.
"It's time to wake up and get ready for school."

Amanda sat up in bed and stretched. Then
she jumped out of bed and twirled around
the room. "I can't wait to see what wonderful
things will happen today," she thought.
"Maybe I will meet a queen—or a fairy—or
even a mermaid! Maybe I will go to a ball!"

Amanda loved to imagine herself doing all
sorts of magical things.

"I know it will be an amazing day!"

"Hmm...What shall I wear today? My ball gown? My jeweled shoes?"

Amanda pulled this and that from her closet. "Oh, and I can't forget my jewels."

She stood in front of the mirror wearing her striped leggings and favorite boots. She looked very ordinary.

But when she closed her eyes and then s..l..o..w..l..y opened them, she didn't see the real Amanda at all. When she used her imagination, she saw herself dressed in a sparkly blue gown, ready to go to a fancy ball.

"Perfect!"

Mommy had Amanda's breakfast on the table—a bowl of cereal and a glass of juice. "Good morning, Amanda."

"Morning!" Amanda twirled to the table, her imaginary ball gown rustling as she walked. She took one look at her ordinary breakfast, closed her eyes, then s..l..o..w..l..y opened them. "Wow!" Instead of cereal and juice, Amanda imagined a table filled with pancakes, waffles, chocolate croissants, cookies and lots of muffins. "Thank you, Mommy, for such a fancy breakfast."

Amanda picked up her orange juice. It was now in a fancy glass.

"Everything is just the way I imagine it to be. What fun!""

Mommy cleared the table. "Don't forget your backpack, Amanda. Daddy will drive you to school today."

As Amanda and Daddy walked to the car, Amanda stopped for a moment. She closed her eyes, then s..l..o..w..l..y opened them. Now she imagined herself being escorted to a fancy white coach drawn by two white horses with rainbow manes.

"Lovely, isn't it, Daddy?"

At school, Daddy waved goodbye.
"Have a good day, honey."

"See you later, Daddy."

The other children were walking down the
path toward the school. How ordinary!

Amanda closed her eyes, then s..l..o..w..l..y opened them—just in time to march along with a big brass band. There were drums, trumpets, trombones and baton twirlers.

"This is so much better!"

Mommy picked Amanda up from school in their SUV.

An SUV was just too ordinary for Amanda. She closed her eyes, then s..l..o..w..l..y opened them.

Now, instead of being in an SUV, Amanda was sure she was driving home in a shiny stretch limousine. The inside was bright pink and very fancy. Amanda poked her head out through the sunroof and waved to all her friends.

Mommy parked in the driveway. Amanda's dog, Teddy, barked and wagged his tail to welcome Amanda home. This was nice, but much too ordinary for Amanda.

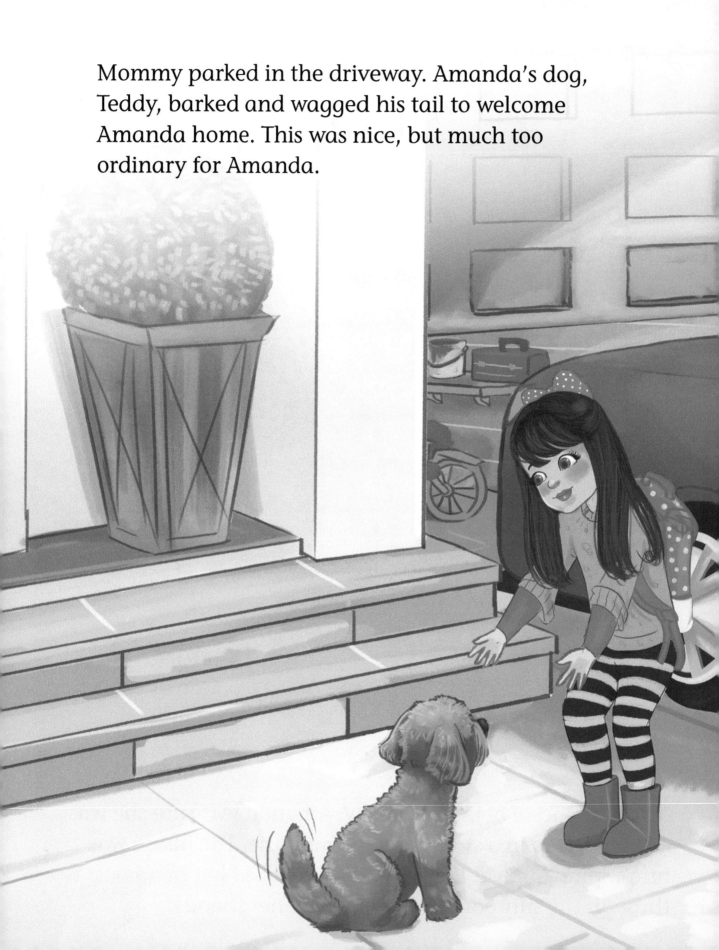

Amanda closed her eyes, then s..l..o..w..l..y opened them. She was now walking across a sparkling drawbridge that led to a big silver castle. Guards stood at attention as Amanda approached. Teddys collar glittered with diamonds.

"You look so fancy, Teddy."

"Okay, honey. Wash your
hands. I'll get your snack,"
said Mommy.

Amanda twirled to the
bathroom, then twirled back
to the kitchen. Peanut butter?
That's so plain and ordinary!
Amanda closed her eyes, then
s..l..o..w..l..y opened them.

Mommy now looked so much nicer in a
puffy white chef's hat and a sparkling
white chef's jacket with pink pearl buttons.
Mommy served Amanda a delicious snack
of fancy cupcakes and lemonade.
"Much better!"

Amanda asked her brother if he wanted to go outside to play. "I'll take the slide and you can have the swing!"

Amanda stopped at the door. She closed her eyes, then s..l..o..w..l..y opened them.

What Amanda now saw in her backyard was her very own carousel, a fancy purple bumper car and a concession stand that served cotton candy—all day!

"Wow! What should I do first?"

Dinner time quickly rolled around. This was Amanda's favorite time of the day. The whole family sat together.

Mommy brought in a BIG bowl of spaghetti and a smaller bowl filled with meatballs. There was a loaf of bread on the table and glasses of milk.

"No! Too, too ordinary!"

Amanda closed her eyes, then s..l..o..w..l..y opened them.

Then she watched the imaginary feast unfold. Amanda now saw plates of food being brought in on silver trays by a waiter wearing white gloves and a black dinner jacket. Gold dishes were placed on a long white table. There were golden candlesticks and even golden goblets. This was definitely fit for a princess.

Everyone in her family was dressed in fancy clothes.

"OH BOY! What a feast!"

"Who wants to watch a movie?" said Daddy.

"I do! I do!" Amanda twirled around the kitchen,
then twirled into the family room.

Watching a movie on a sofa was just too ordinary.
Amanda closed her eyes,
then s..l..o..w..l..y opened them.

Now she was staring at a huge screen, just like in the movie theater. There was a colorful popcorn stand and a cotton candy maker. A nice man, called an usher, offered to help Amanda find a seat in the front row.

At least, that's what Amanda imagined.

"Follow me, ma'am."

"Okay, Amanda, bath time."

Amanda usually takes a bath in an ordinary bathtub, with ordinary soap and ordinary water. Tonight, was different. Before walking into the bathroom, Amanda closed her eyes, then s..l..o..w..l..y opened them.

She stepped into the fancy pink and gold bathtub. Rainbow bubbles floated around her and drifted through the room. Rubber ducks of every color bobbed up and down in the water.

Above the tub was a sparkling crystal light that made the walls glisten.

"This is just what I need at the end of a busy day!"

"Mommy, I had the best time. Thank you for my bath!"

Mommy handed Amanda her blue striped flannel pajamas. "Put these on and hop into bed."

Striped pajamas are just so ordinary. Once again, Amanda closed her eyes, then s..l..o..w..l..y opened them.

She looked down and imagined herself wearing a fancy pink flowing nightgown. It sparkled with jewels of every color. On her feet were fluffy pink slippers, and around her neck she wore a sparkly feather boa. Amanda slid under the covers of her fancy canopy bed. It had the fluffiest white comforter. She loved the pink and white curtains covering the windows.

Mommy came in to say goodnight.

"This is so special!"

This was not an ordinary day. It was filled with sparkling gowns, glimmering bubble baths, fancy horse drawn carriage rides and royal feasts fit for a princess. Amanda was ready to snuggle under her fluffy comforter.

Amanda felt warm and safe and happy. She couldn't *imagine* a more perfect way to end a most *extraordinary* day.

JEANETTE BONFIGLIO is the author of *The Most Extraordinary Ordinary Day*, her first children's book.

She studied elementary education at St. John's University. She enjoys the old classic films of Audrey Hepburn, the charm of the 1950's, and drawn to all things vintage. Jeanette currently lives in Florida among the beautiful palm trees with her husband, two children, and her sweet dog appropriately nicknamed Teddy Bear. All four of them provide endless inspiration.

SHIELA ALEJANDRO is a graduate of Bulacan University in the Philippines where she studied illustration, fine arts, and design. While she is experienced in all areas of design, she has a passion for drawing whimsical illustrations for children's books.

Visit our website for more information and updates about upcoming books.

www.jeanettebonfiglioauthor.com